ANDREAS RIEM & MICHAEL KLEYMANN

FITNESS BOXING

MOVE and BOX

Meyer & Meyer Sport

Original title: Fitnessboxen
© 2008, Meyer & Meyer Verlag
Translated by Heather Ross

British Library Cataloguing in Publication Data
A catalogue record for this book is available from the British Library

Andreas Riem & Michael Kleymann
FITNESS BOXING – move&box®
Maidenhead: Meyer & Meyer Sport (UK) Ltd., 2009
ISBN 978-1-84126-251-2

© 2009 by Meyer & Meyer Sport (UK) Ltd.
Aachen, Adelaide, Auckland, Budapest, Cape Town, Graz, Indianapolis,
Maidenhead, New York, Olten (CH), Singapore, Toronto

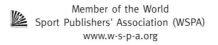
Member of the World
Sport Publishers' Association (WSPA)
www.w-s-p-a.org

Printed and bound by: B.O.S.S Druck und Medien GmbH, Germany
ISBN 978-1-84126-251-2
E-Mail: verlag@m-m-sports.com
www.m-m-sports.com

Contents

C All About Fitness Boxing 59

Recommendations

The classic Olympic sport of Boxing is most definitely not as popular at the grass roots level as it should be. Few clubs offer a broad selection of conditioning, endurance and technique training.

While it is true that the health benefits of boxing training are well-known, I would be delighted if our boxing clubs offered intensive workouts like **move&box®**, fitness boxing or white collar boxing for all ages and abilities, and why not, even in schools. Our licensed coaches are already trained to do this, or they can be trained to do it, as the sports pedagogy and technical exercises are similar. **move&box®** therefore offers a highly recommended fitness workout.

Heinrich Karsten
President, Westphalian Amateur Boxing Association
Vice-President German Boxing Association

The move&box® concept comprises all the elements of a complete boxing workout and can easily be supplemented by leg technique work, which would also make it an all-round workout for kickboxers.

move&box® is less risky than combat boxing, because there is no direct physical contact, but it does focus on punching accuracy, speed strength and dynamism. The training concept uses all the technical components of boxing in order to improve conditioning, endurance, coordination and fine motor skills. It offers a whole body workout that is adapted to the athlete's individual performance level.

The WAKO unreservedly recommends move&box® training for all boxers and kickboxers.

Peter Zaar
President WAKO Germany
(World Association of Kickboxing Organizations)

A   INTRODUCTION

1   Welcome to
move&box®

You grab something, pick something up, walk, jump, bend over, coordinate your movements, and you do it automatically a hundred times a day. You do it correctly, at the right pace, using the right amount of strength and the necessary reflexes. But sometimes we are clumsy and cannot help but notice that our body does not always do what our minds would like and that we also often lack coordination and concentration.

The purpose of any kind of physical training is to increase the repertoire of movement and reaction patterns (so that they are stored in the brain), in order to be able to use/recall them quite automatically. The purpose of every form of physical training is to practice such natural movement forms, to improve them and, at the elite level, additionally to work on particular specific skills. It is important also to stimulate the circulation in order to be able to exercise longer in order to eventually improve conditioning. Endurance and flexibility, along with speed and strength, are important components of conditioning.

move&box® training focuses on achieving perfect physical harmony, litheness, more intensive breathing leading to improved oxygen uptake and reactions. It therefore increases your feeling of well-being, which is the primary goal of a recreational sport.

That is what the authors of this book are aiming for. The exercises should enable you to attain a holistic and all-round natural physical harmony. Another positive effect is the escape from the stresses and strains of everyday life – especially in a fun group atmosphere.

All movement sequences are borrowed from boxing training. The training concept also allows the trainer the freedom to incorporate elements from other combat sports like kick-boxing, karate, taekwondo, and even aerobics, depending on the interests of the class members. The classes are structured according to strict sports pedagogical guidelines and include a warm-up, muscle stretching, partner training, technique training and must finish with a relaxing warm-down. The class should be done to suitable music: the rhythm speeds up as the movements get faster and your pulse rate goes up. In the cool-down, the tempo slows down again and the class ends with relaxation techniques when the music literally fades away. The different types of music run quite naturally one into the other throughout the class.

We explain in the next chapter what makes this workout so beneficial. The basics of flexibility training and particularly how they relate to move&box® training are explained in another chapter. In the final chapters, we try to explain the special place that boxing has occupied in the lives of people of all periods and cultures, why that has always been so and how it has influenced social ideas.

The main section of the book features the exercises in exactly the order that they are performed in a class, along with many illustrations to enhance the explanations. The authors' experience of countless classes with many different types of people has allowed the authors to deliberately choose exercises that people enjoy, so that they make it a kind of fun variation of boxing.

We also show you many exercises that you can do at home. This book is primarily intended for the recreational athlete who wants to keep fit with an activity that is based on the boxing movement repertoire. This can be done alone, but the advantages of a group class are very beneficial, which is why we have focused on this.

This book also gives useful tips for the trainer, helping him to achieve his primary goal, which is to provide those who attend his classes with a feeling of well-being.

Table 1: Demand Profile for Boxers

Core Skills	General Demands
Conditioning	**Endurance:** • General aerobic endurance (improvement and optimization of the cardiovascular system and energy supply)
	Strength: • Maximal strength • Speed strength • Strength endurance
	Speed: • Action and reaction speed
	Mobility: • Flexibility • Stretchability
Coordination	• Linking ability • Orientation ability • Differentiation ability • Reaction ability • Balance ability
Psychological	• Discipline, perseverance • Willingness for exertion • Concentration • Self-control • Self-confidence

Boxing-specific Features

- Endurance rope-jumping or punching training
- Hard punching against sandbags, maize bags or partners
- Endurance rope-jumping or punching training

- Fast, accurate striking of maize bag or mitt

- Constant dodging of opponents' punches or backswings of the maize bag

- Functional coordination of separate partial movements (linking of footwork, body and punching movements)
- Active confrontation with the partner (constant change of distance and position)
- Accurate, delicate execution of partial and whole movements where the strength is well-distributed and situation-appropriate
- Timely and lightning-quick reactions to the partner's actions
- Stable stance, or rather the maintenance and recovery of balance under attack or after quick movements
- Self-discipline when fighting against oneself and a partner
- Controlled and concentrated work/training
- Appropriate reactions to environmental demands

Source: Kürzel & Wastl, Fitnessboxen, 1997

13

2   Fitness and Boxing
Feel good about life

If we wake up in the morning, realize that a new day has begun, and stretch our limbs to prepare our bodies for the activities the day will bring, then we already feel good about life and are fit to face the day. If mind and body are in harmony, we can cope with whatever the day may bring. How depressing if on awakening our joints are stiff, our muscles hurt and our limbs don't do what we ask? The thought of a new day inspires little desire for exciting experiences, so we should do something about it as soon as possible. Yet another reason for some early-morning exercises, and later in the day, perhaps in the evening, also a thorough move&box® workout.

Our first workout is a small, almost silly, but not insignificant test: do we put on our socks and trousers standing up, or do we have to lean on something or even sit on the bed? Getting dressed should be the first test of our balancing skills.

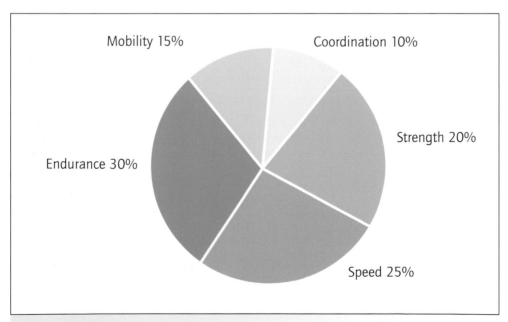

Figure 1: Breakdown of the most important core motor skills in boxing
(derived from Johann & Krempel, 1991, page 381)

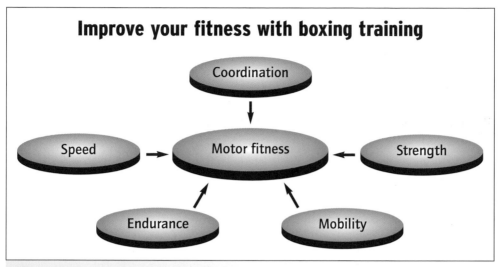

Figure 2: Main components of motor fitness

(after Kürzel & Wastl, 1997)

Balance is one of our most important senses, which we need to walk upright during the day, and particularly if we trip over. It is not uncommon for the elderly to suffer injuries when they trip and fall, but this can be avoided. Coordinated motor skills and lithe mobility give us stability. Statistics show that the risk of falling in old age falls dramatically by 90% in those who do regular exercise until their 50s.

Then comes the journey to work: the last minute sprint for the bus indicates a lack of speed strength, being short of breath indicates a lack of conditioning and stars before your eyes mean you have serious circulation problems. Do you start to sweat if you have to climb only 3 steps? You could take the elevator, but you feel guilty if you take the easy way out. Oh yes, and are you overweight? Every physician says that this significantly increases the risk of heart attack. Do you already know this and still do nothing about it?

No, you overcome your inner couch potato and finally decide to do some exercise – but what kind?

Several sports clubs woo you with plenty of offers that either train endurance (running clubs), build strength (weight training programs), shape your body (legs, bums/buns and tums), improve speed (sprint and jump drills in track and field), practice breathing technique and concentration (Thai Chi) or foster team spirit (ball games).]

It is an uncontested fact of sports medicine that boxing training involves optimal levels of all core motor skills like strength, endurance, speed, mobility and coordination.

Here is an example: if you go on a pleasant bike ride, everyone knows that it is very healthy, but nobody even in their wildest dreams would then think of taking part in the next six-day endurance race for elite cyclists. But boxing only brings to mind the mostly professional world championships fights.

However, for fitness boxing, you need no head protection or gum shield, not even a real opponent, for there is no sparring or fighting, just the benefit of the advantages of the comprehensive workout. There are no nosebleeds and no hooks to the liver area, but instead physical empowerment, personal limit experiences, dynamic processes, followed by a deep sensation of well-being.

The complex movement sequences reduce stress, decrease insulin levels and increase blood flow to the brain by 40%. You lose aggression and become more balanced and relaxed. You awaken your own physical awareness, exercise becomes an adventure, and your improved performance gives a feeling of achievement. That is what a sport should be!

Fitness boxing is suitable for all ages and abilities, for both men and women. move&box® provides a workout for your joints from the ankles, knees, hips, lumbar region, spine, shoulders and neck muscles and quite specifically, the supporting musculature, in a sophisticated developmental program that follows the principles of sports medicine.

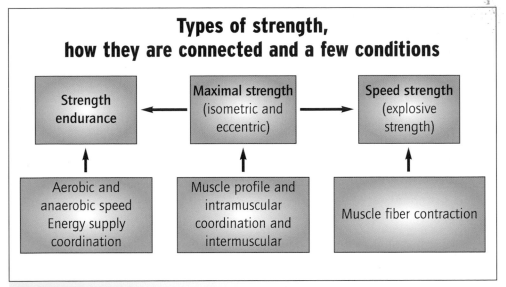

Figure 3: Types of strength (after Grosser, 1989)

The motivations for fitness boxing are as different as the participants themselves:

- Young people. This is their first taste of the sport and they want to learn the movements under the guidance of an experienced trainer. For them it is a first step in a journey that may later lead them to learn "real" boxing – this is how latent potential is discovered.

- Older, active boxers. They can't and don't want to just stop working out after a successful career, for they are passionate about boxing.

- So-called "non-competitors", i.e. wise or cautious people who have realized the benefits of living an active life.

- People who are looking for a different kind of exercise

- Very busy people who do what is called "white collar boxing" just for their personal equilibrium.

Because you are holding this book in your hands and have been interested enough to read this far, you are also one of them.

3 Boxing for Health
Medical background

Doctors, the medical advisors of health insurance companies or healthcare policies are making a concerted effort to persuade as many people as possible to take regular exercise. Studies, especially among the young, show an alarming lack of activity and confirm that seniors who exercise regularly are taking sensible health precautions.

As the old saying goes, any exercise is better than none at all. However, it is true that some sports have rather a one-sided effect on the body and are not necessarily beneficial for everyone. Boxing should not be overlooked in the search for a holistic body workout. *Boxing training is surely one of the most comprehensive whole-body workouts, as it increases circulation to all muscle groups, stretches the body from head to toe, moves all joints functionally, provides an optimal workout for coordination, concentration and reactions and intensively boosts all physical functions. Strength endurance, speed strength and maximal strength are clearly developed in this workout. The training elements of boxing can even be used in rehab sport.* (Dr O. Kinne, Sports Physician). This argument is repeated many times in this book.

A careful exercise program, where the coach, possibly also the primary care physician or sports physician and the athlete take joint responsibility, allows every possible risk of injury to be reduced to the absolute minimum. There is an abundance of specific further training available which the coach, and usually also trainer of the local/regional sports club, can take advantage of to improve his knowledge. In move&box® training too, the utmost importance is attached to the continuing education of the coach, which ensures that amateurs receive the best care possible.

There is a plethora of famous boxers and kickboxers who have managed to keep fit once their fighting career is over because they have continued with their training discipline and their training repertoire afterwards. The most famous of them is probably the German world heavyweight champion Max Schmeling who lived to the ripe old age of 99. Until a few weeks before his death, he trained daily on the ergometer and worked out in the gym several times a week with his physical therapist. Lifelong, conscious self-discipline is undoubtedly the healthiest aspect of this sport.

Finally, a physically active lifestyle allows one to keep fit and keep injuries at bay. This includes a conscious personal hygiene and physical care regime, which aims to increase resilience by establishing a healthy arrangement of day's activities with adequate sleep, work and free time, regular exercise, training and sensible eating habits – in short a healthy daily routine.

The Principle Muscles of the Human Body

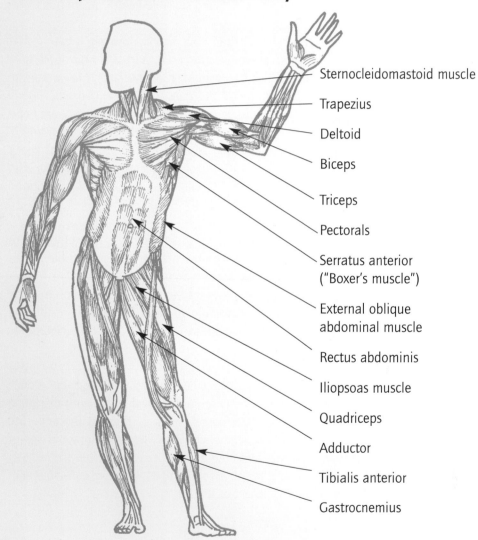

Sternocleidomastoid muscle

Trapezius

Deltoid

Biceps

Triceps

Pectorals

Serratus anterior ("Boxer's muscle")

External oblique abdominal muscle

Rectus abdominis

Iliopsoas muscle

Quadriceps

Adductor

Tibialis anterior

Gastrocnemius

Source: By kind permission of the Regional Sports Association of Northrhine-Westphalia

Figure 4: The principle muscles of the human body - front

However, we should not ignore the fact that every sport has its dangers, boxing included, but in boxing these dangers are clearly limited to combat situations, and as fitness boxing does not involve combat, its risk factors practically zero. However, injuries may occur due to physiologically unsound loading, where incorrect movements can lead to real sports injuries. A typical example of this is a muscle fiber tear, which can turn

The Principle Muscles of the Human Body

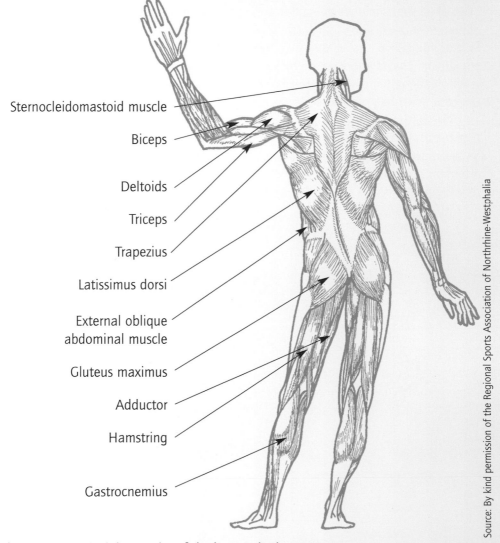

Sternocleidomastoid muscle

Biceps

Deltoids

Triceps

Trapezius

Latissimus dorsi

External oblique
abdominal muscle

Gluteus maximus

Adductor

Hamstring

Gastrocnemius

Source: By kind permission of the Regional Sports Association of Northrhine-Westphalia

Figure 5: The principle muscles of the human body – rear

into a serious muscle injury if it is not handled correctly. This example should remind us that stretching after every warm-up is one of the most important parts of the workout. Muscle cramps (drink mineralized water), strains (ice, rest), fiber tear (training break) and bruises are the most common injuries in fitness boxing. Without physical contact, other typical boxing injuries like black eyes, cuts, nose bleeds, fractures, etc. can be avoided. However, capsular injuries in the bones of the hand (ice, rest, training break) and hand fractures are possible in extreme cases but statistically irrelevant.

50% of all sports injuries affect the legs and 25% the arms. They are usually the result of human error, i.e. due to carelessness or errors of judgment, overtiredness, overloading, lack of discipline, breaching the rules and very occasionally to defective sports equipment. That is also a reason for working out under the guidance of a coach – which is automatic in the case of move&box®. Anyone who practices fitness boxing at home with the punchbag should take extra care.

A prerequisite for taking up fitness boxing is a healthy cardiovascular system, at least an average motivity (which will then be improved by training) and basic mental attention and reaction ability. These skills will then be improved by the personalized training program.

Table 2: Physical Adaptations Caused by Endurance Training

Physical Adaptations Caused by Regular Endurance Training

Musculature

- Improved performance ability
- Increased capillarization
- Increased blood circulation to the working musculature

Heart

- Increased heart weight
- Greater heart volume
- Reduced heart bpm under steady loading
- Resting cardiac output is lower
- Daily cardiac work reduced
- Maximal cardiac output greater

Blood

- Improved flow characteristics
- Increased blood volume
- Increased oxygen transport capacity
- More elastic blood vessels
- Greater oxygen deprivation of the blood in the musculature

Lungs

- Increased lung volume
- Reduced breathing rate
- Increased VO_2 max
- Resting volume increases more slowly in old age

Whole Body

- Immune defense is improved
- Improved metabolism
- Reduced fatigability
- Greater recovery ability
- Reserve capacity is greater
- Slower performance decline in old age
- Bodyweight can be reduced or stabilized
- Improved quality of life and well-being

4   Complex Training Goal
Fundamental building blocks

Have you ever watched an athlete shadowboxing? There is a flow, an unbroken movement with intricate footwork in which all possible jabs and punching combinations are performed – a gymnastic tour de force. The aim is always to enable one movement to flow naturally from the last – that is harmony of movement. Shadowboxing is also a good conditioning workout, because all movements are carried out fast, under control and with high concentration. This fulfills all the requirements for a comprehensive workout: strength and endurance are increased, speed strength is improved with lightning fast movements and mobility exercises improve the body's flexibility. The aim of every fitness boxing course should be the acquisition of excellent, versatile shadowboxing skills, and at the end of a move&box® course, every participant should be able to do this.

Fitness boxing can therefore almost be considered to be a separate sport. General fitness work can also be seen as a component of boxing though, as it is of all other sports. It is all about preparing as many muscles as possible to perform particular, sequential tasks. The circulation should be stimulated, so that the blood pumps the oxygen into the cells to enable the muscles to work. Breathing is controlled and stimulated so that more oxygen can be breathed in, thereby increasing its availability in the blood supply. In the warm-up, the temperature of the muscles is raised so that they are more elastic and can be lengthened and shortened appropriately. In short the right temperature is created to facilitate the metabolic processes within the cells.

The tendons are also carefully stretched as far as possible to increase their range of motion. And last but not least, post workout relaxation exercises ensure that our body (musculature, circulation, breathing) is rested, relaxed and able to go about its daily work better than before. Our fitness is therefore improved and we feel better about ourselves.

All these processes are highly complex, although they happen quite naturally. We often don't realize how important they are to us until they go wrong. It is precisely to avoid this that we practice sports, in this case a methodically sophisticated boxing workout.

Details and individual exercises are shown in the chapter on warming up (Chapter 7). Below are just a few guidelines.

Muscle Use in Boxing
Muscle Chain Throughout the Body

Participating Muscles:

Pectoralis major
Serratus anterior
External oblique abdominal
Trapezius
Infraspinatus
Large rhomboid
Latissimus dorsi
Lumbar muscles
Teres major
Triceps
Anconeus
Biceps
Biceps
Coracobrachialis
Brachioradialis
Extensor carpi radialis longus
Extensor carpi radialis brevis
Flexor carpi ulnaris
Extensor digitorum
Gluteus maximus
Gluteus medius
Tensor fasciae latae
Fascia lata
Great adductor muscle
Gracilis muscle
Sartorius muscle
Rectus femoris

External thigh muscle
Inner thigh muscle
Hamstring
Semimembranosus
Semitendinosus
Pes anserinus insertion
Gastrocnemius
Soleus
Achilles tendon
Tibialis anterior
Extensor digitorum longus
Extensor digitorum brevis
Peronaeus longus
Peronaeus brevis
Flexor digitorum longus

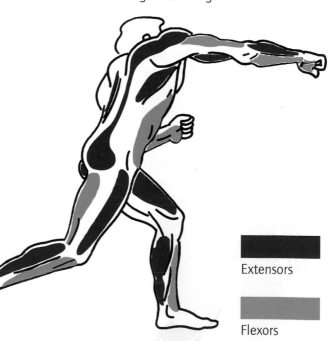

Extensors

Flexors

Figure 6: Muscle use in Boxing

Basic Training Principles

After the initial acquisition of movement skills, the purpose of every exercise program is to improve them further either to maintain them at recreational sports level or to improve them at elite level. This process is only possible if the training stimuli are strong and long-lasting enough to trigger adaptation processes. Sports scientists say that the stimulus shapes the organ, i.e. the tissue becomes better and better structured for its purpose. By working harder, the qualitative constitution of the organs changes and their specific efficiency is increased (basic morphological law). Well-known examples are the athlete's heart, which increases in size as a reaction to increased loading, or the athlete's lungs, whose ability to absorb oxygen increases enabling more oxygen to be supplied to the blood.

move&box® is less concerned with fatigue resistance ability (which is the preserve of special endurance training), and more with flexibility, strength and speed, i.e. those skills that, along with endurance, are components of conditioning. Flexibility is gained by coordinating muscle activity with balance.

We need strength for every movement; without strength we couldn't even walk upright. Muscle strength in a healthy person is sufficient for day-to-day conditions. If I increase these by training, my strength increases very quickly, but is also lost just as quickly if I stop training. Speed depends on the coordination of a mental impulse with an appropriate stimulation of the relevant muscle concerned. This can also be trained. For example, everyone knows the jumping jacks sequence: clap the hands above the head, then on both thighs, then behind the body, on both thighs, then in front of the body, on both thighs and again above the head... The task is understood in the head, but it is quite hard to do in practice, until a rhythm, an automatism is established. Then the exercise can be performed more and more quickly. Automatisms are very important in boxing movement sequences (compare changing gear and engaging the clutch when driving – for beginners these are a real feat of coordination, for experienced drivers a natural process that needs no reflection). Punching combinations become so engrained that they are mechanical, in which case gaps may open up where effective single punches can be landed.

Supercompensation

Performance improvement is an important requirement of every form of exercise, hence the inclusion here of a graph that illustrates a fundamentally important concept. Our graph of a workout shows that with every training load we slightly exceed our existing performance threshold. The fatigue this creates then makes our performance level drop significantly. Then a recovery phase sets in, which clearly raises the athlete's performance threshold above its previous level, and increases it (overadaptation). If a new training stimulus is introduced at exactly this point, the performance threshold can be gradually increased, giving rise to an increase in functionality and performance. Sports scientists call this law **Supercompensation**.

This concept is a prerequisite of a sophisticated exercise program, and should form the basis of all sporting activity.

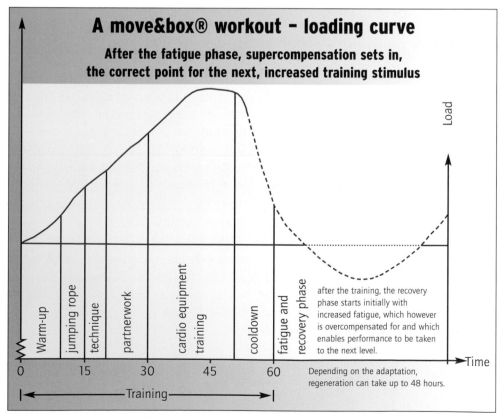

Figure 7: Supercompensation

5 Mini Boxing Academy
A general introduction

We should start by knowing what we want to achieve, by having a goal. In boxing, this would be *suppleness*, *nimble footwork* forward, backward and sideways, *dodging* in the typical boxing *defensive* stance sometimes upright, sometimes bent over forward or backward, physical orientation at different levels, having loose shoulders that allow us to *push* our arms forward while *guarding* our head and chin; and finally, that all of this happens automatically in a fluid interaction. Such automatisms (like when driving a car the combination of braking, releasing the clutch, engaging a gear, engaging the clutch, pushing down on the accelerator – everything happens automatically and by itself), can only be learnt by practice, practice and more practice...This is exactly what we do, we break down *complex actions* into small, partial steps so that eventually we can manage the whole movement.

Footwork

This is the most important component of boxing. Because man walks upright, movement always involves a sequence of steps – and this is already very relevant to boxing. But it is not enough just to take one first step, as we just stand there wobbling, rather as if we are standing on an unsteady ship: therefore, stand with your feet shoulder-width apart, the left foot (for left-handed people the right foot) a good foot length in front. That is a stable stance that we can test quite easily by shifting our bodyweight forward and backward and right and left all the while maintaining the basic stance.

Such a stable stance is not only important if the surface underfoot is unstable or the body is unsteady, but it facilitates quick forward, backward and sideways movements. The foot placed to the front, rear or side is shifted further forward, backward or sideways and the gap from the rear foot is kept exactly the same. In the final position, after such a sequence of steps, both feet should adopt the starting position once more, i.e. feet shoulder-width apart and the front foot half a step-length in front.

For these small steps to become automatic, first take several steps forward. Your rear foot should never be further forward than the front one, and vice versa when moving backward: the front foot never overtakes the rear foot – and to the side: the right foot never overtakes the left and vice versa. The stance with feet shoulder-width apart and one foot a foot-length in front of the other should always be maintained. In this way, you learn how to make use of space. The competitive boxer needs to use this feeling to be able to move around the ring as though in his sleep; moving backward to avoid being forced into a corner, and dodging to the side when required.

So, move in a square, one foot forward, one to the left, one backward, one to the right – you should now be back in the starting position. The whole thing can also be done with three steps forward, three to the left, three backward and three to the right etc. Repeat with increasingly quick steps, now combine the step sequences freely with each other as above, loosely, with no tension and soon you will master the boxer's typical footwork.

Basic stance

Straight Right/Cross

Stand at an angle with one leg and the corresponding shoulder and hips slightly forward. Both hands are held at chin-height. Extend the hand above the front leg further forward, while the rear hand touches the chin. The front hand is called the lead hand and serves mainly to gauge the distance, then shoots out again and again like a snake's tongue in order to engage with the partner (also double punch), to unbalance him and to stop him using his own tactics. You can use it to make gaps in his cover, where you can then land a powerful punch with the rear hand.

When extending out the lead hand, make sure that this goes out horizontally straight in front of you and is retracted at least as fast (if not faster) again on the same trajectory (do not let it drop) in order to provide immediate cover for the face again. The shoulders should be relaxed and raised a little in order to protect the side of the chin from the opponent's hook.

Straight lead hand

Straight rear hand

The hips should also be twisted slightly in the punching direction, so that the bodyweight increases the punching force and the distance is covered exactly – perfect.

The movement sequence of the other hand is in principle the same, but just a little more difficult, because it is the rear hand above the rear foot. The distance to the opponent is somewhat greater and therefore the hips must be twisted further forward. You will automatically raise the heels of the rear foot and notice how your bodyweight automatically shifts over the front foot. By simultaneously turning the hips forward and straightening the rear leg, the punch will be even stronger (bodyweight makes a big difference).

Both the lead and the rear hand fists should always be slightly turned forward during the punching action, so that the bones of the index and middle fingers meet the object (first the punchbag, ultimately the opponent). Again, bring the hands back to the head more quickly than they were punched out as this is the only way to gain complete protection from your opponent's counter punches. Now also try to regulate the punching strength, as in fitness boxing the aim is not to knock someone out but to perform controlled, dynamic movements. The best way to practice these punching exercises is against a punchbag that you can easily prepare by placing a mattress upright against the wall or winding a floor mat around a pillar. For this exercise, *boxing gloves* should be worn (ideally bag gloves).

Combination straight and footwork

Imagine you punch forward with the lead hand at 1, then at 2 you retract it again. Also at 1 you bring the front foot half a step forward and bring the rear foot back at 2. And now you put both things together. So, on 1 you punch your lead hand forward and simultaneously put your front foot forward, on 2 you pull your arm back and put your rear foot back – so easy! You can do this in almost the same way moving sideways or backward. Next, you can practice moving the front foot forward while simultaneously shooting the punching hand forward – it goes almost in a cross and consequently it is also called a diagonal step (as opposed to a linear step in which the lead hand and the front leg are moved at the same time). After breaking the movement down in the numbered steps 1 and 2 for learning purposes, you can then create a flowing and dynamic movement. It is best to practice it in front of the mirror – it sounds more difficult than it is, which is why learning by doing makes it easy!

Hook

There are eight types of hook in boxing, horizontal hooks to the left of the head and body, right of the head and body and the uppercut with lead and rear hands to the head (chin) or body (solar plexus). Starting from the basic stance with the arms close together (elbows near each other in front of the body), lower your left elbow so that our arm is horizontally bent, and then by twisting our hips and slightly turning our front foot inward (lifting our heel in the process thereby shifting our bodyweight) punch into the opponent's body, and then return to the starting position. That is the **lead hand hook**. The **rear hand hook** is done in exactly the same way, by turning the rear foot slightly inward and bringing the rear hip forward. To punch the body with the hook, we must dip down by slightly bending the knees; the punching technique (fist and elbows parallel, i.e. horizontal) maintains balance. It works!

Lead hand hook to the head   *Rear hand hook to the body*

Rear hand uppercut

Both **uppercuts** are a lot more difficult. There are various techniques for learning them. In the starting position the knees are slightly bent, and almost springy. To get even lower, for the left uppercut we turn the whole upper body slightly to the left (the right knee bends toward the left knee). The subsequent push-through of the left leg allows for a powerful upward movement, and we now use this upward swing in order to pull out the left fist in the direction of the opponent's lower costal arch or chin, two very important knock out points. We then do the same thing with the rear hand. Don't forget to raise the shoulder of the outward moving hand at the same time as the punching movement in order to protect the chin and the side of the head.

Another variant teaches that the right rear arm is lowered slightly and the right elbow and hips are brought back, so that by then shifting the balance onto the left leg and lifting the heels of the right leg the fist strikes the target. What sounds complicated becomes a natural, fluent swing with practice.

This can take up to six months to perfect, so don't despair if you can't do everything as well as your coach's demonstration to start with.

All of these typical boxing movements are also incorporated into fitness boxing classes. The active boxer now requires months, if not years of practicing punching sequences and punching combinations that are formed from these basic movements. Reaction skills and conditioning must also be improved. What sounds easy requires great diligence, strict discipline and great mental and physical effort. That is why boxing cannot be learnt in a short course of a few weeks and has remained a fringe sport at elite level. However, as it is excellent training for all the muscles, joints, circulation and even the mind, the training basics are ideally suited for a recreational sport, which is what this book is all about.

Defense Against Punches

Your opponent's best punch is the one that doesn't hit you – that is one of the most important nuggets of boxing wisdom. That is why the teaching and practicing of defense is a priority in the boxing academy. The fact that my opponent can defend himself gives me the right to fight against him. Otherwise a fight would be immoral. All defensive movements require lightning fast reactions and fast muscle movements and are therefore also a valuable component of fitness boxing.

Parries: the opponent's straight punch (whether with the lead or rear hand) is most easily intercepted with the inside of the fist – if the opponent punches with the lead (e.g. left) hand, I intercept this with my rear hand (i.e. my right hand), by letting it hit my slightly opened inner glove with a little counter-pressure. I am now in a very good position to counter the punch with my own straight lead hand.

There is another way of deflecting the punch from the opponent's rear hand, which is

Two-handed cover-up

Slip to the left

to divert the opponent's straight punch from outside to inside with my rear hand or inner arm, sometimes also punching under his fist in order to guide it upward instead of hitting me. In the case of a hook, I can also do this with the outside of my arm.

Blocking: However, for punches from the half and near distance, defensive guard simply involves bringing the elbows together in front of the body to protect the stomach and the side of the body concerned and by moving the hips slightly and protecting the face or the side of the head with quick, short movements of the hands. This is how the boxer protects himself. Another type of guard is the shoulder block, i.e. a raised shoulder, which serves to protect the boxer - usually combined with a straight punch from the same side – which automatically protects the chin and the jaw from a side hook.

Parrying the opponent's lead hand

Inward redirection of the opponent's lead hand

Covering up or blocking therefore just mean intercepting the opponent's punches with parts of the body other than those the punch was intended to hit.

Slipping and ducking are other defensive styles. It is essential to train the upper body to move in all directions, particularly backward, and to move the feet while turning the hips. Someone who has a good feeling for distance knows very well from experience whether he can avoid a straight punch with a dodging movement, and very elastic knee joints are required for the quick vertical ducking movements. Constant movement in all directions (*swaying* - upper body movement, *active footwork, bobbing and weaving* - lateral bending of the trunk, *ducking* - sidestepping the punching direction and dipping under the punch) is the best defense, because it means that the opponent's target is constantly moving. Nothing is more dangerous than boxing a barely moving sandbag, nothing more difficult than boxing a ceaselessly moving opponent. That is also a reason why the lighter weight boxers' fighting style is usually more technically demanding with intensive footwork and ceaseless punching combinations and the heavier classes usually feature more powerful single punches.

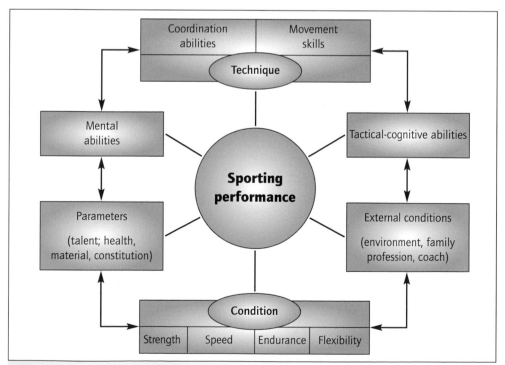

Figure 8: Essential components of sporting performance (from: Ehlenz et al., 1987)

The reader suspects why most boxers need months if not years of experience in order to be sure they can protect themselves; but also that good defense makes the risk of injury lower and lower. That is why defense is still the best protection in boxing.

B   Main Section
move&box®

6   Training Groups and Facilities

Not every gym is equipped with a wall mirror and the finest sports floor; some sports clubs make do with a simple sports hall. This has nothing to do with the quality of the teaching. However, there are facilities which show the participant how much attention their gym or club pay to the move&box® classes they offer.

These are the availability of adequate hi-fi equipment, good acoustics in the training room, a training surface that is large enough to accommodate the number of students in the class and with ventilation that guarantees sufficient oxygen supply for a sweat-inducing sport. The lighting is also important. An even illumination (artificial light) of the whole training surface, ideally directly from above (no shadows) is preferable. Laterally falling natural light (dazzling glare), particularly from direct sunlight, can be very annoying, and the trainer should definitely make use of blinds if they are available.

A fitness boxer knows the importance of checking that footwork and arm movements are coordinated, so they don't like to be without a mirror for shadowboxing. This kind of personal checking is also desirable in a group setting. One is able not only to watch oneself, but can also be oriented by how others are moving. The trainer must always be clearly visible, especially during the warm-up, for he leads the way. If there is a wall mirror available, he can even stand with his back to his students, in which he case he takes one step to the left on his left side. However, if he stands facing the class he must remember to reverse left and right in his own actions, which requires a great deal of coordination ability on the part of the trainer himself.

The class participants also want to build up friendly relationships with each other, for this is what makes communal training really fun. This can sometimes be achieved in totally mixed (gender, age, ability, social status) groups, although it is usually easier to group people by age – it is up to the class organizer trainer. The athletes should wear sports kit (solid sneakers with shock absorption in the ball of the foot and in the heel area as well as good rolling properties are particularly important) as well as gloves that have been specially developed for move&box® training. These may be purchased or borrowed from the gym/club. Hand bandages or wraps are recommended to immobilize the metacarpal bones and the wrist, but also to soak up sweat. They are very cheap to buy in shops or in

move&box® glove – hitting surface

catalogues – in emergencies cotton gloves are also acceptable (for protection). Finally, the coach also needs a timer, which monitors the lap times with a acoustic signal. And then you're all ready to.....

7   Warm-up

The warm-up is divided into several sections. It can start with running in different directions (sideways, backwards, etc.), and also with running exercises in place (including high knees, shifting bodyweight, etc.) First the circulation should be stimulated until the body starts to sweat. Then follows a special warm-up that already starts to imitate typical boxing movements. This can be followed by exercises from head to toe (foot, knee, hips, shoulder area). Once the body is warmed up, it is very important to carry out stretching exercises. The conventional method is to do three (or more) repetitions of a stretch, each time with stronger pressure lasting a few seconds – modern research tells us that it is not advisable to bounce in the stretch. The shoulders, hips and feet are also stretched. After this, there should be a short rest (drink, wipe away sweat, etc.)

1. Pull both arms horizontally backward and forward.

2. Pull both arms vertically backward and forward.

3. Arm circling.

4. Cross hands in front of the body.

1.   Lift the feet behind the body to practice balancing and train the leg muscles.

2.   Raise the knee until the thigh is horizontal – here until it touches the outstretched palm of the hand. This is the logical counter-exercise to the previous one.

3. + 4.   Swing the feet forward and to the side, encouraging conscious posture control.

8   Jumping Rope

The aim of this part of the workout is primarily to improve endurance. It is increasingly falling out of favor with some athletes, but this should not be the case and it is the trainer's job to insist on it, depending on the fitness levels of the group. But who wants to run out of steam after just a little exertion? So, let's get to work. Apart from the fact that jumping rope is also particularly good for perfecting footwork, one can hold the rope in the hand specifically to train the wrist or the shoulders with wide swings above the head (lasso). If someone exceptionally has to miss a class, he can still do this part of the workout – a rope fits into any travel bag. Once you have mastered the art of jumping rope, you will enjoy it more and more. There are so many possible moves that you can even develop your own workout and turn it into a show, which always goes down well with the public at sports galas.

1.   Arrange the rope in a circle on the floor and walk around it in half steps sideways – here to the left, holding your right hand out palm down. Then change sides.

2. + 3. The rope is stretched out on the floor, and you can perform various stepping and jumping exercises over it.

4.   Swinging a rope is a fantastic way of training the wrists.
Don't forget to turn the wrist forward and backward and to change hands.

5.   Jumping rope is one of the most popular endurance exercises in boxing training.

6.   Bending the knees, not the upper body, side steps, then standing up straight again are all important forms of footwork training for the boxer.

7.   Two people hold the rope at different heights and a third person performs a variety of different jumping exercises.

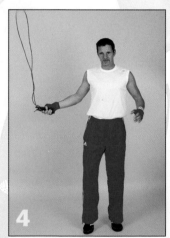

9   Technique

Technique is of fundamental importance in competitive boxing, and it also has its place in move&box®. Punches and their coordination with footwork require practice and training. Advice on how to do this can be found in the chapter "Mini Boxing School" (Chapter 5). Each workout can focus on selected leg or punching exercises and this can be expanded upon with subsequent partner work and cardio training. This gives a structure to the whole course. Depending on the level of difficulty, performance accuracy and also on how much time is available, 5-10 minutes can be dedicated to technique. The correct technical performance of the movement gives a better and better sensation, strengthens concentration and also trains the eye – significant results that should not be renounced. For this part of the workout, slow music that does not break the concentration is the best accompaniment.

1. General basic stance for fitness boxing – the basic boxing stance involves holding the arms/elbows more closely together (with the fist right next to the chin) and bending the knees more, there is more bounce in the knees and the head is kept down (chin nearer to the chest). Right-handed athletes stand with the left foot in front = normal stance, southpaws with the right foot in front; the lead hand is at the front and the rear hand at the back.

2. The Jab (straight left) is then performed with the lead hand. It is important that the punching arm is kept horizontal and straight (long-distance punch), with a twisted fist position so that the opponent is hit with the first two metacarpals.

3. The punch (straight right) is performed with the stronger rear hand. The right shoulder is raised to cover the side of the head and the opposite shoulder drops down, the hips turn with the movement.

4. In the left uppercut, the left arm is slightly lowered, in order to then aim a punch at the opponent's head or body. The right fist takes over responsibility for protecting the face.

5. In the right uppercut, the inward twist is very important, as the punching power comes from the straightening of the rear leg. In both uppercuts (right and left), the shoulders are raised to protect the side of the face.

6. + 7. Both hooks are performed absolutely horizontally to the opponent's head. In the process the heel of the foot below the punching hand is raised and usually also turned slightly outward.

8. Here the athlete bobs (always to the outside) to avoid an intended straight punch from the opponent's dominant hand. It is more common to bob to the opposite side to avoid the more common punch from the lead hand.

10   Partner Training

There are various partner training exercises that can improve strength, increase awareness of regulatory processes, and improve coordination. These include dipping under the partner's arm, partner abdominal exercises, bobbing and weaving step and arm exercises, shadowing the partner while they move in different directions, games with opposite footwork (stepping on the feet or moving the feet out of the way), pushing each other out of the way (with the arms placed on the shoulders) and many more.

1.   Partner A moves his right lead hand over the head of partner B, who dips by bending the knees and then stands up again. The same thing is repeated with the left lead hand. Then A and B swap over.

2. + 3.   An exercise that requires coordination and concentration. From the starting position (photo 2), the partners alternately step to the right (photo 3) and left.

4. With two half-steps to the left (and then to the right), partner B dips under the outstretched arms of partner A and back again, sometimes between the arms, to the left of the arms, between the arms, to the right of the arms – then A and B swap over.

5. + 6. With rhythmic hip twisting movements, the partners clap their opposite hands together. This can also be done with the inside of the feet. The two exercises can then be combined.

11   Cardio Training

This is the main part of the workout and what the athlete now does increases the efficiency of his cardiovascular system and improves his coordination. There should be 15-20 minutes of circuit training. Partners should change after each circuit or at least after every section of the workout. This makes for a much more comprehensive workout, for a better understanding between the class members and a more varied class – every change represents a new challenge. The focus of this part of the workout is the improvement of the technique training, corrections by the trainer are still important. The

Correct
move&box® glove positions

1.   Position for straight fists.

2.   Position for hooks.

3.   Strengthened double position for uppercuts.

trainer demonstrates the exercises that are to be performed, e.g. lead hand (lh) of partner A into the lead hand of partner B, the same with the rear hand (rh), constantly alternating lh / rh, double punch with only one hand, the same with the side hook and uppercut – always at the marked target on the inside of the hand of the boxing glove. Gradually, steps forward and backward are added, and then steps to the side, in order to gain spatial awareness during free movement. Once these are mastered, combinations can also be introduced (like mitt training in boxing) with a partner. That is almost like sparring and very close to "real" boxing. Circuit times can be 45 – 60 seconds for the untrained, while fitter individuals can manage up to 2 minutes. With shadowboxing, active rests can also be programmed, and its length and frequency should be adapted to the group. The music can be freely chosen, but it should be motivating.

1. + 2. As with all mitt work, diagonal punches are landed in the outstretched glove of the partner. Here the lead hand straight punch (jab) into the left, or rear hand straight punch into the right hand of the partner.

3. + 4. The female partner throws a left uppercut into the male partner's crossed hands, and he pushes back. The partners then swap roles and also alternate between lead hand and rear hand punches.

5. + 6. It is also easy to practice the side hook. The female partner holds her opened hand out to the side, so that it is hit exactly on the inside of the glove. If one partner punches harder, both gloves can be held against each other (also at different heights) and they should aim to hit the top of the gloves.

12 Cool Down

The purpose of an active recovery is to stabilize the circulation, return the pulse rate back to normal and bring the body temperature back to a healthy starting level. This is achieved with easy, gentle movements to calm, relaxing music. Relaxation exercises can be done on mats (avoid a hollow back) or standing, focusing on concentrated deep breathing. Avoid lowering your head below your waist at all costs. The leg and calf musculature, the hip flexor and spinal erector muscles, lumbar spine, chest and lateral trunk musculature should also be stretched in this phase.

1.   The Achilles tendon is stretched by placing one foot on the floor quite far behind the body, keeping the heel flat on the floor while inclining the upper body forward slightly. This exercise can also be done in front of a wall.

2.   Pull the heel up toward the bottom, which should clearly be felt in the quads.

3.   Bend forward with a straight back, while maintaining the tension in the abdominal muscles, as this also recruits the back musculature.

4. Stretching, by placing the hand above the head (and possibly bending the corresponding hip), the other hand is held low in front of the body to increase concentration.

5. Here the athlete is stretching her right shoulder by pushing her outstretched left arm into the body with her left arm. Perform the same exercise for the left shoulder.

6. Raise your right arm above your head and place the right hand between the shoulder blades. The exercise stretches the triceps.

7. Stretch the muscles of the side of the neck by tilting the head to the side and simultaneously pulling down the opposite arm.

13   Reflection

Reflection should follow every workout. This means a conscious post-workout assessment of how it went. Every participant is unique and has a different motivation. He initially needs encouragement, and then careful, sensitive criticism. The trainer must have praise for everyone: what has he done well? Where did he show particular commitment? When did he integrate well? That has a much more motivating effect on the athletes than scathing criticism. The whole point is to cultivate, develop and encourage skills. If a person does not possess a certain quality, even the most intensive training will not bring it out.

Reflection also provides a good opportunity to question particular sensitive areas and to gain a better understanding of the athlete. This also allows the trainer to obtain indispensable feedback.

The athletes are made aware of what was done in the workout so that the logic behind it becomes clear. This already gives some ideas for the next workout, and possibly also for any training that can be done at home in the meantime (e.g. conditioning running, exercises, strength training). Every participant should be personally addressed once before the end of the class. This is an indispensable part of a group class; it creates an enthusiastic atmosphere and helps the athletes to identify with their sport.

C   All About Fitness Boxing

14   Choice of Music
Setting the mood

Hearing is one of our most important senses. The perception of acoustic signals and transfer of these impulses into motivation is also one of our basic coordination tasks. Competitive dancing is undoubtedly a sport, and it has many parallels with boxing. Music is also one of the main features of many forms of exercise, e.g. classic aerobics or Tae-Bo. In move&box®, too, music creates a good atmosphere in which people can work out with more relaxation and grace. At least in the warm-up and cooldown, music is consciously chosen to support the movement, it determines the rhythm and pace of the activity. That is initially easier than one might think.

What effect does music have? It motivates, it releases emotions and brings relaxation. The choice of music is determined by two criteria, speed and style, i.e. the quicker the rhythm, the more intensive the movement pattern that goes with it. Personal musical tastes vary from rock, pop, latin or techno, and the choice depends on the course participants. The atmosphere should always be good, which is why the choice of music also involves constantly balancing the preferences of the coach and the athletes.

Hard, clear beats are suitable for boxing. If the music is too melodic, everything becomes more dance-like and motivation can suffer. Melodic tones are suitable for relaxation; some people even prefer the sensuality of Tai Chi or Yoga music. Participants also subconsciously adapt to the volume. In the technique section, the volume should be quiet enough for the trainer's instructions and corrections to be heard, and at the end of the class, it should be turned down very low, and the trainer's comments should be reduced to a minimum also. As for the sound quality, original CDs sound better and they should be handled with care. The sound is also better from good quality hi-fi equipment, which is now actually standard equipment in good gyms and clubs. Pitch control allows for better adaptability and flexibility.

Table 3: BPM and Type of Music in Fitness Boxing

Training module	Type of music	BPM
Warm-up	Motivating	125-135
Jumping rope	Flowing, strong beat	130-150
Technique	Clear, slow	110-120
Partner work	Lively	130-145
Equipment – cardio	Harder beats, house, rock, charts	130-150
Cooldown	Relaxing, calm	100-120
Post workout stretch	Asian music	*

* no BPM requirement for relaxation music

Music always has a structure; pop and chart music is usually composed in **4/4** time. Beats are familiar to everyone who taps their fingers or toes when listening to their favorite song, and we learn at school that every piece of music is always divided into beats. The **beat** is the smallest counting unit in music. A movement sequence with eight steps is a **phrase**. Four phrases made up of 32 beats form a musical arc. At the end of a musical arc there is a noticeable loss of tension. The first beat is emphasized and this is the point at which an exercise starts or changes. Movement sequences that can be divided into two, four or eight steps are ideal for training to music in 4/4 time.

A piece of music in 4/4 time can also be run at different speeds, in which case the beats per minute are different. The music for the warm-up starts more slowly and at some point the bpm are increased, then the music really speeds up and in the cooldown phase at the end of the workout, the music becomes slower and more relaxing again.

Bpm information always appears on special cds that are sold for aerobics. Warm-ups usually start with 125 and increase to 135 bpm. The rhythm increases up to 150 bpm in the main section of the workout to get the circulation going and promote sweating, and later falls to below 120 bpm, while music without a beat is suitable for stretching and relaxing at the end of the workout.

In Thai Boxing, the music that may sound strange to our ears symbolizes the cut and thrust of the combat and serves to motivate the athlete accordingly. Music is capable of far more than entertaining; it can guide, accompany, regulate and relax. Music that provides the soundtrack for training must be deliberately selected though, there is no place for background music from a radio station in a move&box® class.

No.	Title I Artist	BPM	Time
01	Intro I m-e-m		00:12
02	Superfreak I Countdown Media Coverversion	135	03:34
03	Jump I Madonna	135	04:02
04	Nothing In This World I Paris Hilton	136	03:46
05	People Always Talk About The Weather Yonderboi	137	03:30
06	Martyr I Depeche Mode	138	04:38
07	Champion Sound I Fatboy Slim	139	04:11
08	Moving Too Fast I Supafly Inc.	140	03:55
09	Call On Me I Janet & Nelly	140	03:40
10	Ring The Alarm I Beyoncé	140	04:34
11	Self Control I Infernal	141	04:32
12	Everytime We Touch I Cascada	142	04:04
13	Eye Of The Tiger I Crew 7	143	04:02
14	U & Ur Hand I P!nk	144	03:47
15	I Don't Remember I Northern Lite	145	03:52
16	Me & U I Cassie		03:11
17	Numb I Pet Shop Boys		03:26
	Total:		62:55

Trackcard for your CD-Bag

music in motion

Order No: PL-AE14
www.tunes4sports.de

Source: The Audio Factory Production, Publisher and Trading Company, 2006
www.tunes4sports.de

Figure 9: Example of background music for a move&box® class

15 Sample Class Format
move&box® class

Phase	Reps.	Duration	Description
Warm-Up			
	16 right/left	32 beats	Walking in place
125-130	16 right/left	32 beats	Outside/inside march
bpm	16	32 beats	Outside march plus arms open (arms below horizontal)
ca. 10 . min	16	32 beats	Outside march plus arms open (Lower arms vertical)
	16 right	2 x 32 beats	Crossed arms, in front of the chest (hips turned inwards)
	16 left		
	16 right	2 x 32 beats	Arms crossed, backwards on the shoulder
	16 left		
	8 left/right	32 beats	Hands grip in front
	8 left/right	32 beats	Hands grip in front, diagonally high
	16 left	2 x 32 beats	Leg curl
	16 right		
	2 x 4 left/right	32 beats	
	4 x 2 left/right	32 beats	
	16 left/right	32 beats	
	16 left/right	32 beats	Leg curl plus jab
	16 left/right	2 x 32 beats	Jab
	16 left/right	2 x 32 beats	Punch
	16 left/right	2 x 32 beats	Upper cut
	16 left/right	2 x 32 beats	Hook
	left	2 x 32 beats	Knee lift
	16 right		
	16 left	2 x 32 beats	Knee lift plus arm pull
	16 right		
	8 left/right	16 beats	Tap front
	8 left/right	16 beats	Tap side

Phase	Reps.	Duration	Description
	16 4x4	32 beats	Tap front
	16 2x2	32 beats	Tap side
	16 2x2	2x32 beats	Front kick low
Jumping			*Lay rope on the floor*
rope		2x32 beats	Dancing around the rope right/left
135 bpm		2x32 beats	
		4x32 beats	Variations right/left
ca. 7 min.			
	8		*Straight rope*
	8	2x32 beats	Step touch
	8	2x32 beats	Jump
	8	2x32 beats	Tap diagonally forward
		2x32 beats	Jump
			Participants can also drop the jumping
		32 beats	*Take the rope with the right hand*
		32 beats	Rope swinging (right)
		32 beats	Rope swinging (right) plus small skip
		32 beats	Rope swinging (left)
		32 beats	Rope swinging (right)
		32 beats	Rope swinging (left/right)
		4x32 beats	Jumping rope (easy jump)
Technique			
	16	32 beats	Boxer position forward slide (to the left)
~110 bpm	3 x 16	3 x 32 beats	Jab – front straight left
	16	32 beats	Boxing position forward slide (to the right)
6 min.	3 x 16	3 x 32 beats	Jab – front straight right
	16	32 beats	Boxing position, forward slide (to the left) engaging hips
	3 x 16	3 x 32 beats	Punch – right rear straight
	16	32 beats	Boxing position, slide forward (to the left) engaging hips
	3 x 16	3 x 32 beats	Punch – left rear straight

Phase	Reps.	Duration	Description
	16	32 beats	Left jab
	3 x 16	3 x 32 beats	Left jab, right punch
	16	32 beats	Right jab
	3 x 16	3 x 32 beats	Right jab, left punch
Partner work			
	4 x 8	32 beats	Partner A: 2 x squat
135 –	4 x reps		Partner B: 2 x arm swinging
140 bpm			*Alternate*
4 min.	4 x 8	32 beats	Side tap right; arms outstretched
	4 x reps		Legs together, clap partner's hands
			Side tap left, arms outstretched, legs together, clap partner's hands
	4 x 8	32 beats	*Partners now face each other?* Partner B: arms stretched out forward
			Partner A: dips to the left, center and then the right
Cardio			
	4 minutes		Left jab
135-150 bpm	4 x 1 min.	alternating	Right jab
	5 minutes		Jab – left/right punch
25 min.	1 min. shadow-boxing		Jab – right/left punch
	5 minutes		Jab – punch – jab
	1 min. shadow-boxing		
	4x1 min	alternating	

Phase	Reps.	Duration	Description
	5 minutes		Jab – punch – squat
	1 min. shadow-boxing		Punch
	4 x 1 min	alternating	
Cooldown + stretching			
			Remove gloves while walking loosely
		2 x 32 beats	Tap front shaking out arms
- 100 bpm		2 x 32 beats	Tap side shaking our arms
		2 x 32 beats	Tap back shaking out arms
			Breathing exercises
Stretching	No bpm		• calf / chest
			• hip flexors
			• hamstrings
			• erector spinae
			• lateral trunk musculature
			• triceps
			• neck muscles
			Finish with breathing exercises

16 Sandbags etc.
All types of training equipment

"Real" boxing is not just sparring with the partner in the ring and does not always involve physical contact with the special risks that this entails; "real" boxing means all physical training that prepares for, maintains and increases physical fitness. A few typical examples of this are exercises using the maize bag, punching ball and sandbag, which are an essential part of every boxer's training.

The sandbag is really the essential piece of boxing equipment. It allows the development of the ability to gauge distance, of punching power, of the individual punches, of combinations and also the footwork required for attacking and finishing off a punch. In addition, it can be used to practice evasive and dodging movements, or even conditioning and endurance. You can take out your aggression on the sandbag, talk to it, conquer it – it is your best, quietest and most patient partner!

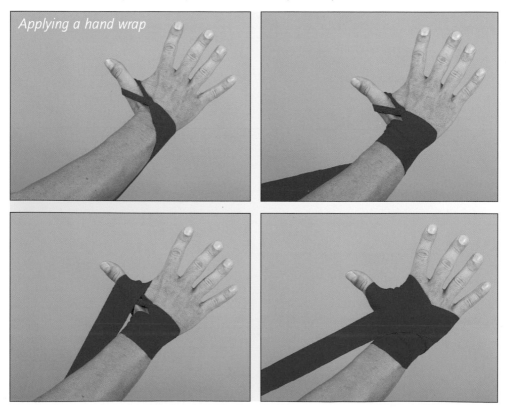

Applying a hand wrap

As training at the sandbag is at least as hard on the wrists, knuckles and thumbs as a fight, the hands must be carefully bandaged beforehand. It is silly to just slip on a pair of boxing gloves and throw a few punches. The wraps also absorb sweat from the hands and stop the inside of the glove from getting dirty quickly. According to the regulations of the German Amateur Boxing Federation, the length of the wrap should be no longer than 98.5 inches and no wider than 2 inches. Wrapping a bandage requires calmness and is something of a ritual. Each person does it differently, but the important thing is that the wrist, metacarpals and MCP joint are immobilized. People usually start at the wrist, then wrap each finger separately, then wrap around the wrist again, then around the knuckles and the palm of the hand. This ritual also gives you the time to prepare mentally for the stress of the coming workout.

Gloves are the next consideration. If you work out regularly with the sandbag, you need what are called **ball gloves**. They are special gloves that give protection from skin abrasions with padding that distributes the stress of the continuous punches, but

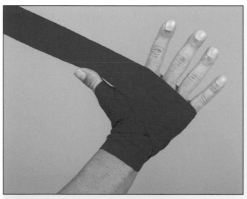
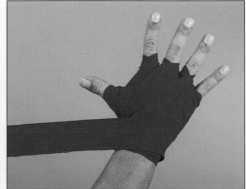
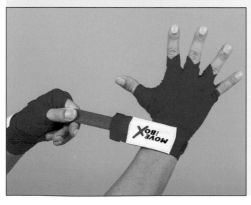

they are not as cumbersome as sparring gloves. Some are stitched to allow the addition of extra weights. They are usually much more expensive, but you are advised to purchase them.

Sandbags themselves come in all shapes and sizes. They are usually between 20 inches and 5 feet 10 inches high and their weight varies correspondingly too. Some are angled at the bottom and are specially designed to practice uppercuts. Some are covered with expensive materials (linen, nylon, even strong artificial leather), and classically also still with leather, but this has little to do with the durability but more to do with image and naturally affects the price. The notion that they are filled with sand is only a rumor – if this were the case, it would be just like punching a concrete block. They are actually filled with compressed material, horsehair and felt. Well-equipped gyms are increasingly equipped with a variety of sandbags to suit boxers of different sizes, statures and ages and of differing strengths.

Gloves, jump rope, bandage

The sandbag

You should alternate between them to vary your training (punching power, speed and rate).

The way the sandbag swings depends mainly on the punching frequency, it imitates the movements of the fictitious opponent. The athlete must therefore already have a certain amount of experience with fighting against an opponent, so that he is able to use his imagination. It is then possible to practice counterpunches, sidesteps, punching to the body and the head, the extension of the rear hand and the feeling for round times. The sandbag is the all-round training apparatus par excellence for the boxer.

Wall punching pads cannot move and are not as versatile. They are very useful when practicing punching accuracy. Pyramid-shaped, firmly mounted wall pads are more suitable for practicing the hook and the uppercut. In clubs, floor mats are often just placed against the wall, fixed with a strap and then used as a punching pad. Then the hook can also be practiced by just standing almost at right-angles to the mat, which is very useful for beginner's group work. It is more difficult to practice coordination with

Wall punching pad

footwork, but it can be trained by standing further away from the mat, intensive attacking with small boxing steps and gauging the right distance for long jabs.

The **maize bag** is the most useful piece of equipment for learning to gauge distance. It is constantly swinging and demands great mobility from the athlete, especially lateral mobility (many people find boxing more difficult when moving from side to side than when moving forward or backward). When a punch is landed properly and it barely moves, it means that the punch was made from exactly the right distance away (the same length as our outstretched arm). This equipment is also very suitable for practicing counterattacks, or for practicing bobbing and weaving or other defensive techniques using smooth punches.

The monotonous clattering of the usually leather **platform speedbag** forms a rhythmic background noise in the gym. On the count of one, we punch, on the counts of two and three we hear the sound of the bag hitting the platform.

To start with, the tempo can be moderate; punch 2 x right and 2 x left (other sequences are always possible). Only when you have mastered this should the tempo be raised. Soon the pelting of the speedbag will become your personal trademark. This is impressive and also fun, even though it takes a while to learn.

Punchballs and **floor to ceiling balls** are other types of equipment, which are particularly useful for training the eye and punching accuracy. The double end bag is particularly useful for training speed and mobility (dodging techniques). Some trainers think that these two pieces of equipment are only suitable for practicing skills, not for boxing-specific use. However, there is no doubt that the punch bag is a vital piece of training equipment.

The **jump rope** has always been part of the boxer's kit. Jumping rope should also be an indispensable part of the fitness athlete's cardio workout.

Maize bag

A shaped sandbag is more versatile

Floor to ceiling ball

We should not need to describe its versatility here, because everyone knows how to use it. It is a multi-functional piece of equipment not only for the familiar skipping exercises, but it can also be swung to train the wrists or high above the head (lasso swinging) to mobilize the shoulder girdle. The traditional form of jumping rope is not necessarily more important, but can be a useful workout for home training and when traveling.

In move&box® training, special **mitt gloves** are used for partner training, which is quite similar to the actual fighting process. They are our most important piece of equipment in intensive cardio-technique training. They allow for a very realistic simulation of punching accuracy, coordination, punching combinations (moving all the while) plus a constant switching between attacking and counterattacking. These gloves combine the advantages of a training mitt (which is only worn by the trainer) with two-way close combat, and exercises for punching and defensive techniques.

Similar gloves are available from various manufacturers. The additional internal hand padding makes them a little heavier though. The special gloves, like other combat gloves, weigh only 10 oz.

move&box® gloves

The so-called hand mitt is very versatile and allows the wearer to present different punching points. It enables the practice of optimal punching accuracy.

17   Home Training
Selected exercises

What is the fitness boxer's most important requirement for home training? The simple answer is: willpower! Nowhere is the need for individual initiative greater than in unsupervised training situations, and unfortunately, this is when our inner couch potato tends to take over. Home training is no replacement for boxing classes with a trainer. However, it is a very good supplement, and a good way of reflecting on what has been learnt in class and keeping oneself limber until the next class in the gym or club.

As far as facilities are concerned, all that is needed is an open space of a few square yards, with enough space to stretch out the arms, take a few boxing steps and lie stretched out on a floor mat. Anyone who has set up a gym at home is very lucky, but this is not essential and the cost can be prohibitive. My tip is go to the flea market and there you will find a lot of sports equipment that you could use at home for your private fitness workout. In this way, I personally have gradually accumulated a weight bench, an ergometer bike, a few dumbbells, an elastic band (Theraband), a stepper and a punching ball for less than $70.00.

Every athlete has his own training program that can be supplemented by training at home. If you attend classes 3 times a week, you can quite safely do exercises every morning (it is hard to overdo this), and if in addition you also do technique work like strength training, that is quite sufficient. You can also add endurance training, e.g. a

From the flea market (or the classified ads in the newspaper) a viable home gym can be equipped for as little as $70.00.

gentle one-hour jog or a 3,000-yard run in a time below 20 minutes. Perhaps you would also enjoy sitting on the exercise bike in front of the TV and cycling for a couple of hours. Even on holiday there is always room for a jump rope in your luggage – jumping rope is the boxer's most important cardio workout. Don't forget to leave two training-free recovery days, usually the weekend, as the body needs time to recover. The basic idea to bear in mind is not to overdo it and to vary your workouts so that training is fun.

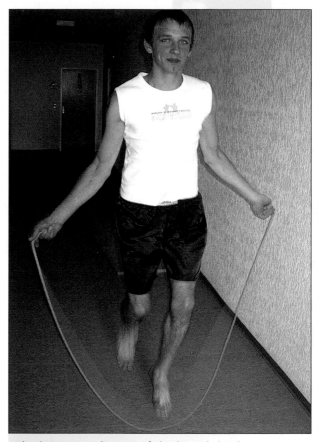

The jump rope is part of the boxer's basic equipment for the essential cardio training.

Like every other workout, training at home always starts with a warm-up. Listen to fast-paced music on the radio or, even better, play an aerobics CD and you will soon get into the swing. Start easily and slowly with walking in place and stepping forward, backward and to the sides. To loosen the joints, we work upward from the ankles via the knees, hips, shoulders, not forgetting to loosen the neck muscles, and then back down again.

The exercises get more and more demanding, dynamic and faster and increase the circulation higher and higher, warming up the whole body in the process. So here are a few suggestions to get you started.

Stage 1: Raise the left foot, circle the ankle then repeat with the right foot. Then raise the knee until the top of the thigh is horizontal and circle the lower leg (or move your foot in a figure-8 pattern, which loosens the hip joint). Repeat on the other leg and in both directions. Then turn the hips, with your hands on your sides (your head should be vertically above your feet and as still as possible). It is very important for boxers to have a loose shoulder girdle. Raise your shoulders, lower them and circle them forward and backward, circle your arms (with a small, then increasingly bigger, then smaller amplitude). Let your head fall alternately on your right and the left shoulders. Bring your chin down to your chest and tilt your head back – now we've reached the top...

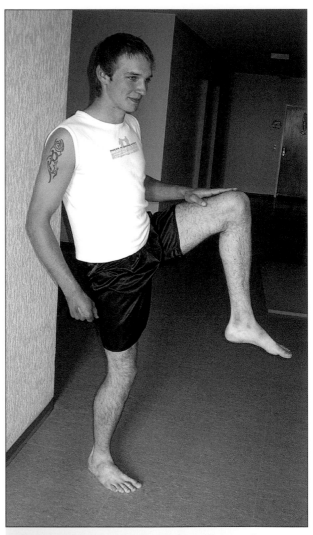

Hold the thigh in a horizontal position and move the lower leg in a circular pattern; this exercise trains balance and flexibility.

Get your circulation going by raising your knee, then the tips of your toes, up to the horizontal palm of your hand.

Now we work back down to the feet again. Firstly alternating throw your lead hand and rear hand forward, raise them vertically then slowly lower them again, then also stretch them across your body to the side (never bend the wrists). Now raise your knee up to your horizontally outstretched hand, several times to the left and then to the right. Then repeat with straight legs, i.e. raising the tips of the toes to the outstretched hands. You should now be breaking into a sweat. Now you could also raise alternate heels to your glutes.

Now we have reached the feet again, we practice shifting balance by doing alternate jumping exercises on the front and rear legs (boxing basic position). You can do two-legged forward and backward jumps in the same stance. This brings a physiologically sound warm-up to a close.

Stage 2: Shadowboxing, ideally in front of a large wall mirror: practice all the punches, i.e. lead hand straight, rear hand straight, hooks: lead hand and rear hand to body and head, uppercuts: lead hand and punching hand to body and head as well as all combinations and variations. In the combinations, it is important to imagine oneself in a realistic combat situation. Therefore, combine e.g. punches from long distance (straights) with punches from the mid-distance (hooks), in order to close in on the imaginary opponent (take steps toward him), in order to finally tackle a straight punch from your opponent (usually involving taking a step backward). You can set the level of difficulty yourself, depending on how you feel on the day, your pulse should reach 180 bpm though. Never let your inner couch potato get the better of you!

The great thing about fitness boxing is that there are no downsides, it is not dangerous and it not only gives you a workout for your whole body, but also trains your self-discipline and your mind.

Shadowboxing is the cornerstone of fitness boxing. It requires conditioning, the coordination of arm movements and footwork, concentration on pure technique and mental effort is required to perform a fluid exercise sequence.

Stage 3: Now comes the time to work on our strength. That can be a series of quick straight punches by the lead and rear hand for 30 seconds, a 30 second rest, then the next set for e.g. a total of 5 reps.

Push-ups should be performed with calm intensity. Here: stay low, bounce a little and look right and left keeping a smile on your face.

Or you can torture yourself with push-ups – the first set easy, then the second set with the hands facing forward then backward, the third set with alternating hand position. In the fourth set, stop pushing and stay in a low position and just bounce a little, look left, look right, left, right and then push up again with speed and strength. If you are able to clap your hands after pushing up quickly – good for you! Those are very challenging exercises that clearly show us where our limitations lie.

Crunches to tone up the abs also belong in this training stage, as do lateral leg raises. You can make the exercise more difficult by supporting yourself with the arm under your body and raising your hips.

Raise your hips and bounce the top foot up and down; this is a great exercise for training general body tension and the lateral abs in particular.

Another suitable exercise for this stage is to lie down on your back and raise and lower your straightened legs. You can also circle your legs with your feet together in the same direction to the right and then the left, or circle each leg in a different direction at the same time. Abducting and adducting the legs several times (without letting them touch the floor) is another popular

Circling both legs to the right and left strengthens the abs and improves hip flexibility.

exercise – these are all good exercises. There are also plenty of exercise ideas to be found in books or magazines on fitness.

The following exercise is a great transition to the next stage: go down on all fours, i.e. support yourself on your knees and the palms of your hands. Extend your right arm to the front while you extend your left leg horizontally to the rear then vice versa – a great strengthening exercise for the back.

On all fours, switch between the cat position (arched back) and a flat back to strengthen your back and improve balance.

To increase the difficulty, after extending the arms and legs, bring the elbows and knees together under the body and arch your back. But make sure you carefully stretch out your back again afterwards, and hold the position briefly. This is a very beneficial movement sequence.

Stage 4: Never neglect your stretching exercises. Achilles tendons (take a step forward with your heels on the ground, the rear leg bent, support the hands against a wall), lower back musculature (bend over at the hips keeping the upper body horizontal), lateral hip bends (hold). Lunges should be familiar to everyone. Then stretch your arms back by standing sideways on to a wall and/or pulling one arm in front of the upper body to the opposite side with the other hand wrapped around it, stretch the neck muscles (look backward over your shoulder) – again a whole variety of possible exercises. NB: either hold the stretch for several seconds or relax slightl after a few seconds and then stretch

Stretching the shoulder girdle next to the wall (backward) or in front of the body (forward) increases flexibility.

It is very important for boxers to train the neck muscles (stretch them by looking back over your shoulder) in order to be able to absorb the opponent's punches to the head.

again. Also repeat the stretching exercises several times. Stretching increases flexibility, one of the most important prerequisites for boxing.

Stretching Methods

- **Static Stretch**
  A sustained stretch in a particular position ("holding") for a normal period of from 10-15 seconds to a limit of up to two minutes; 6 – 10 reps.

- **Intermittent Stretch**
  Slow stretching and holding of the stretch stimulus in the final position. After a short pause, adopt the same stretch position and stretch to the final position again and hold for 15-20 seconds; 10 seconds rest; 6 – 10 reps.

- **Proprioceptive Neuromuscular Facilitation Stretch (PNF)**
  (also called contract-relax stretching or CR)
  The muscle to be stretched is maximally isometrically contracted (contraction) and held for 10 seconds (hold); the tension in the muscle dissolves (relax); 10 seconds stretch; 6-10 reps.

- **Dynamic Stretch**
  Slow, careful, rhythmic bouncing movements with small range of motion in the maximal joint position. 20 seconds duration (ca. 20 bouncing movements); 10 seconds pause; 6-10 reps.

Stage 5: As in a class situation, when training at home we should also finish with a cooldown. Shaking out, relaxation and deep breathing are the order of the day. You should also take the time to reflect for a moment and to ask yourself whether you enjoyed the exercises in the workout and found them beneficial. Here, beneficial means that our flexibility and boxing technique have improved. The physical exhaustion disappears and becomes the joyful anticipation of the next workout – with our training group or home alone once more – good job!

Return your circulation back to normal by breathing deeply.

18 Fitness Boxing in Gyms
A modern workout for differing requirements

In both clubs and gyms, the sheer quantity of combat sports and styles on offer can be confusing. It is not surprising that athletes often change their minds. They may try out another sport in the same club, or they may even change their gym altogether. Who benefits from this? Nobody can benefit from this kind of instability caused by an excess of choice – on the contrary, it contradicts the ideals of combat sports, i.e. discipline, patience, stability and perseverance, just as it does the goals of every sport where perfection can only be achieved after years of training. **Children, young people** or **beginners**, who experience setbacks in combat sports training (as they are occasionally difficult), very soon lose interest and give up. To avoid this happening, before putting them in challenging combat situations, they should first have a thorough athletic and technical grounding.

Intensive fitness boxing fits the bill. Setbacks are inevitable in any sport and should not be an excuse to give it up. This is an important lesson for pupils and parents alike. The proprietors of most gyms are always on the lookout for new exercise classes to offer recreational athletes, for the latest trend. But these are just passing fads, and Boxaerobics will go out of fashion just as quickly as Tae-Bo® did.

However, fitness boxing can be classed as a real sport and definitely as the most important introduction to combat sports (see also chapter 4 "Complex Training Goals"). It offers an introduction to boxing for beginners, but is also totally suitable as a training supplement for elite boxers. Fitness boxing is also quite suitable both for kids and seniors – it is up to each gym to decide which target groups they will run classes for.

In the classical boxing clubs or gyms, which exist to turn out **elite athletes**, naturally competition-oriented training is available and the athletes are "cultivated" for as long as they can compete at elite level. At some point they can no longer keep up this level and soon their interest in boxing also disappears. It should never get to this stage, where someone who has paid their dues is no longer wanted.

By just keeping fit, the "non-competitors" can still get a lot of enjoyment out of the sport. The same is true for boxing, kickboxing, karate and combat sports in general in a form that takes away the pressure to perform, minimizes the risk of injury, can be practiced individually and allows the athlete to continue to enjoy training. All of these aspirations are shared by the best-trained athlete and the novice recreational athlete in a move&box® class.

There is therefore no need for any trendy new sports, for this concept already exists in the form of move&box®. It is particularly suitable because it retains the classical workout structure of a warm-up, technique, partner training, mitt training with specially boxing gloves and cooldown, and trainers are therefore quick to trust it. It flows because the exercises are done to selected music (see chapter 14), as you may already be familiar with in aerobics, though without a set choreography, in which case the people at the front of the class may quickly be shown up. The concept is classical, because it uses the typical boxing and kickboxing motor skills, and is also versatile, because, depending on the trainer's skill and knowledge of the participants, elements of all combat sports can be integrated – anything is possible within reason.

Very important: this concept requires no expensive new equipment. The sole expense is the purchase of special boxing gloves (see chapter 15). This cost is either included in the course fee, in which case the gloves are provided free of charge, or the athlete is recommended to buy them as part of his kit as well as his tracksuit trousers and sneakers – a third possibility is to have an appropriate number of pairs of gloves available to borrow in the gym. That is the best solution in the case of several parallel-running courses, or if move&box® shows are used to advertise a gym somewhere else. A move&box® course is therefore totally affordable. An invaluable advantage is that one does not necessarily need a sports hall (often they are all completely booked out by other sports clubs). A well ventilated room will suffice, because no fixed installations are necessary, apart from a power connection for the CD-player, and changing and showering facilities.

More and more sports clubs and gyms are offering this attractive form of recreational boxing training, and giving them the chance to acquire a healthy lifestyle, as advocated in the introduction greeting by the President of WAKO and WABV.

But move&box® is not only one exercise class among many offered by gyms. For boxing clubs it represents an opportunity to run it as a course and to charge a fixed price for it, which not only opens up a new source of income for the organizers, but also means that the participants do not need to be club members. This is exactly what the boxing section in my club does, enabling it to finance acquisitions for the boxing section that it would not be able to do on membership subscriptions alone.

Such courses are currently not only offered by gyms or sports clubs. Some cultivate collaborations with adult education colleges, rehab centers or health insurance companies, as fitness boxing is very well-suited for their winter programs. It is essential though that the trainer has the necessary competence, at least an instructor's license and a solid physical education background.

19 Boxing
A classical sport

We are all familiar with the word boxing. For a great many fans, the fights of the German boxing idol Max Schmeling or the most elegant of boxers, Cassius Clay who became a legend as Mohammed Ali are unforgettable. Then there are those charismatic athletes who have become mythical figures like Jack Dempsey, Joe Louis, Rocky Marciano, Sugar Ray Robinson and George Foreman, without forgetting the brash Mike Tyson and his nemesis Evander Holyfield. But we also still remember the fights of the younger boxers on the European scene like Henry Maske, Axel Schulz and Darius Michalszewski and Sven Ottke. Fights by the Klitschko brothers Vitali and Vladimir, Felix Sturm, Markus Beyer or the boxing great Nikolai Valuev stimulate the arguments of experts and passionate fans alike.

All aspects of boxing are discussed, passionate support or uncompromising rejection are commonplace. A person who actually practices the sport definitely sees it differently than a spectator. This sport provokes emotions and allows us to participate in experiences that were occasions of important celebrations in ancient cultures. They are almost ritual debaucheries — in any case this is how the journalist Michael Kohtes sees it — in which all fear of normal prohibitions disappears. *For what inspires us with fear and shocks our consciousness can also cause rapture, even ecstasy*, he wrote (see bibliography). It is therefore not surprising that for boxers themselves and also its passionate spectators, the art of boxing is imbued with something almost supernatural.

It is impossible to trace the origins of boxing, the "simple science," for it is a product of the natural instinct for self-defense or self-protection — which we all still possess today. It is an innate reflex to defend oneself by holding out one's hands, and that is turned into a sport — you extend your arms in front of you, your elbow is straightened, as this is the only way that the arm can withstand maximal frontal force. The boxer makes use of this, for if he also uses his bodyweight e.g. by twisting his body into the punch while extending his arm (in boxing, the lead hand straight is called the jab, and the rear hand straight is called a straight punch), he can use maximal force on his target and therefore throw a powerful punch.

The origins of boxing can be traced to the fighting practices proper to every region of the world and every society. It is therefore commonly believed that the martial art of boxing is traditionally related to methods of self-defense or warlike confrontation. However, there are also scientists who are convinced that ritual activities are the origin of all sporting activity, and that even the Olympic Games can be traced to pre-Doric fertility rites (*Drees* and *Diem*). Others (*Eichel*, *Lukas*) see an original, instinctive link between sporting activity and the work. Nowadays, sports scientists focus increasingly on the function of sporting activity as an escape valve, as a source of fun for a society with leisure time on its hands. This is exactly where fitness boxing comes in.

Boxing in Africa, America and Asia

In **West** and **South Africa**, there are representations of boxers in prehistoric cave paintings. Ancient rock paintings showing boxers with bandaged fists can be found in Rhodesia/Zimbabwe. The first known modern African boxing school was opened in Kimberley in 1878.

On the **North American continent** we know that the Native Indians played combat games, but these were more similar to wrestling. We hardly need mention that the USA is now a boxing stronghold, although kickboxing was not introduced in the USA until the 1970s.

Since the 11th Century, Burmese boxing, similar to Thai Boxing, has flourished in Asia. In the Nagai Pagodas there are pictures of two boxers wearing the sarong (longyi) typical of the time. The martial arts in China have a history going back several thousands of years. The Shaolin monk Bodhidharma (around 520 BC) founded Shaolin Boxing, which aimed for the harmonious development of body and mind. After the Boxer Rebellion of 1900, Chinese Boxing was forbidden, but it continued to be taught underground – so that it has now developed into an activity widely practiced by the general public, like fitness boxing.

In India, the sport was influenced by Hellenism. Marriageable daughters were fought over by suitors in the boxing ring. In a cave in Ajanta, there are boxing scenes that originate from 200 BC.

Boxing in Ancient Greece

In the areas influenced by the commerce and politics of ancient Greece (Hellas), all sports were very popular with the public, particularly the combat sports. Superhuman abilities were attributed to the athletes and gods themselves were heroes.

Heracles, the son of Zeus, was the very model of hard training and an ascetic lifestyle; he became the patron of gymnasts. He was said to have founded the Olympic Games. Or what about Atlas, a divine strength athlete who had to bear the weight of the earth day after day, and don't forget Apollo, a real lover of competition − he was particularly skilled at fighting with his fists and is therefore the original model of the boxer. That is why he was chosen to be the patron saint of fighters.

Homer makes several mentions of the art of self defense, of the fame that fighters achieved with only the strength of their arms and legs, and who is the greatest, as he described in his "Odyssey." Facial scars caused by

Greek boxer with "sharp thongs." The fighter's face shows the traces of his injuries: a cauliflower ear and a broken nose
Bronze statue, 1st Century BC.
Museo Nazionale Romano delle Terme 1055.

fighting injuries were considered honorable and were displayed with pride. In Athens, the upper classes were called *those with the beaten ear* (we would now call this "cauliflower ear"). It was the visible proof of their enthusiasm for boxing. Anyone who emerged victorious from one of the national festivals of Olympia, Delphi, Corinth or Nemea acquired immortal glory and was a national hero. Fights went on interrupted, sometimes for days on end until the decision was made. The targets of the attacks were mainly the opponent's head; body blows were frowned upon, the clinch made the fight hard and heated.

It forced people to box from a defensive position. In Ancient Greece, boxing was a sport for the general fitness of the population, not only a competitive sport or a form of training for the military. That it produced Olympian heroes who were the stuff of myth is a sign of esteem and high respect.

Gladiatorial Fights in Ancient Rome

Things changed completely in Ancient Rome. What in Ancient Greece was revered as a perfect union of mind and body did not survive here. There the sacred sport gradually became a bloody popular spectacle. The Roman fist fighters degenerated into objects of public sensation mongering. Otherwise the gladiatorial combats were nothing to write home about. The author M.B. Poliakoff wrote: *instead of providing a means of self-expression and competition, the arenas above all displayed the power and controlling force of their organizers...the crowd learned that the Caesar was the referee with the power of life and death. They saw others dying with the approval of the state and therefore felt both relief at their own survival in that gruesome world and also a great fear of the authorities. A modern analysis of the arena states that: "on the psychological level, the gladiatorial combats provided a stage where power and tragedy could be witnessed...whatever happened in the arena, the spectators were always on the side of the victors."*

In Rome, the games took place for the first time in the year 263 BC. They were initially arranged for military purposes and were soon regular components of the Roman festival program. In 29 BC, in Rome the first amphitheater was built out of stone to emulate those in Campania. Nearly every significant town in the provinces soon had such a building. Numerous ruins have survived, like the arena of Verona and a few in towns in the south of France like Nîmes. However they were all surpassed by the Colosseum built by the Caesars of the Flavian house in Rome.

The gladiators were recruited from the criminal ranks, war prisoners, slaves or acquired Freemen. They were imprisoned in barracks or gladiator schools. Discipline was strict in the schools; the severest of punishments were meted out even for small misdemeanors. However, they were well-cared for physically thanks to a healthy, regimented lifestyle and plentiful diet. They were trained by socially well-positioned coaches.

Initially they fought with weapons, swords, occasionally even with visor helmets and shields, but their chests were always bare. If a gladiator was wounded to the point of no longer being able to fight, he laid down his shield and stuck up a finger on his left hand. If the public liked him, they indicated by holding their thumbs up that he should be allowed to leave the fight, otherwise they gave the thumbs down to make the gesture of death. The vanquished gladiator received the mortal blow. Slaves took the dead bodies through the gate of the goddess Libitina into the mortuary chamber, while the victor triumphantly brandished the palm branch that was presented to him.

In boxing history, this combination of the fascination of death and sadistic mass ecstasy has never been more obvious than in the times of the gladiators. It is therefore only logical that the Roman Catholic Church, as guardians of Christian morality, banned fist fighting as a result. Christ was concerned with spiritual salvation, not physical comfort, and even more controversially, the human body soon became considered to be the source of evil, lust and sin. This ensured that every notion of athleticism disappeared from scholasticism. A fatal error, which ensured that it took more than a thousand years until boxing could again be freely practiced in the West.

20   Boxing
An established combat sport

At the end of the 17th Century, fist fighters started cropping up again at local fairs. They fought over *Prize Fights*, especially in England. They were prize fights that still were more like brawling. However, fist law increasingly became the means of defending or improving one's status. The oldest confirmed source of such a prize fight dates from the year 1681; a London newspaper, *The Protestant Mercury*, reported on a fight between a lacky and the master of the London Slaughterhouse.

The term boxing has been understood as *to fight with the fists = to box* since 1694. The first boxing school in England was run by the athlete James Figg, who was definitely a boxing champion of his time. He possessed a show booth and there he also taught the boxing-mad sons of London's ruling/upper classes. However, it is another Englishman who is considered to be the father of modern boxing, his name was Jack Broughton, a giant of a man. His well-honed technique and his fair play in the fight already aroused admiration, and he already tried to establish a set of regulations. He called his training academy in Tottenham Court Road *The Mystery of Boxing*. However it was no palatial academy, but just a modest training room behind a pub. The competitive passion that was emerging in London society and the hunger for adventure and experience meant that the time was right for boxing.

Around 1800, John Jackson, a respected boxer, ran another boxing school in London that was frequented by pupils from the best houses in London. The Prince Regent and later King of England George IV also studied the art of boxing there. Another prominent pupil was Lord George Gordon Byron, an ecstatic poet and a boxing romantic. For him, boxing meant confronting the challenges and adversities of reality (he was physically handicapped by a stiff leg), not letting himself be defeated by setbacks, but getting back on the offensive at the next opportunity and in this way developing a unique, distinctive, nonconformist style. He was an extravagant maverick. The authors Kohr and Krauss remind us that boxing was first organized in the year 1812, at the *Pugilist Club* in London. London was also the source of the reforms that led to the sport of boxing we know today. They are based on the London Rules of 1838 and those of the Marquess of Queensberry of 1867.

Intellectual Self-Awareness

As proof of the confusion surrounding boxing, its ambivalent status at the turn of the century was demonstrated at the 1896 Olympiad in Athens, when the organizing committee did not yet include boxing as a sport, while eight years later on the occasion of the 1904 Olympiad in boxing-crazy St. Louis in the USA, boxing was included this time. For the 1912 Games in Sweden, the sport was again canceled, this time because the national laws of Sweden considered boxing to be brutal and placed a general ban on the sport. Since 1920 though, boxing has been an Olympic sport.

MAX SCHMELING vs JOE LOUIS
· YANKEE STADIUM · NEW YORK ·
JUNE 18, 1936   ·   OFFICIAL PROGRAM 25¢

The poster for the fight on June 18th. German statisticians date the fight on June 19th based on Central European Time.

The first German boxing club, SV Astoria, was founded in Berlin in 1912. An unprecedented fascination with boxing began, centered not in London, but Berlin and Paris. Throughout Europe, soon poets, thinkers and scholars were addressing the topic of the sport of boxing. It was a time when people were looking for heroes and role models and aspired to be them themselves. The intellectuals enjoyed it; the Bohemians of the time wanted to be around the boxers. At first, boxing matches were just part of variety shows, or the circus, as described above. This also explains how boxers came to frequent artists and actors in the 1920s and 1930s. As Max Schmeling said: *artists, take me to your heart, for boxing also is an art.*

In 1927, Max Schmeling, the German and European Champion, was the darling of the Berlin smart set, which he had not sought but tolerated. He came into contact with the greatest gallery owners of the Weimar Republic, e.g. Alfred Flechtheim, with painters like George Grosz, dancers like Anita Berber and many other artists (he also sat as a torso model for the sculptor Rudolf Belling). Ultimately, this acceptance into society also allowed him to meet and fall in love with the actress Anny Ondra, whom he soon married and lived happily with for 55 years. No wonder that the politicians of the coming generation, i.e. the Third Reich, increasingly sought out the company of such heroes, role models were in demand. Max Schmeling also allowed them to admire him, but was never corrupted by them.

The spirit of optimism of the start of the new century was made for novels like The Abysmal Brute and The Game by the best-selling author Jack London – he himself had stood in the ring many times and knew the milieu and could describe very accurately the boxer's search for courage and willpower – he was a boxing romantic. *It was the search for the lost wilderness, the return to the experience of elemental self assertion, which London found in a fair fist fight*, wrote M. Kohtes. Another passionate advocate of fist law was the future Nobel Prize winner, the Flemmish poet and playwright Maurice Maeterlinck, who, along with other sports and a weakness for motorbikes, also took up boxing training in 1906. His Eulogy on Boxing was a much respected hymn to the sport of boxing. He still boxed as a 50 year-old on the occasion of a benefit performance against the future cruiser weight world champion Georges Carpentier.

One of the most distinguished poets of modern boxing was Ernest Hemingway. He boxed in his youth in Kansas City and later in Chicago and also occasionally earned extra income as a sparring partner. True to his spontaneous nature, he once even won a show fight against a professional boxer on a ship's passage from America to Paris in 1921, in which he made a fool of him using every trick in the book. Hemingway was obsessed with boxing and in Paris too could not get his boxing gloves on enough sparring partners and enjoyed his reputation as cold-blooded, manly and heroic in the face of pain and danger. A literary critic, M. Kohtes, once stated: *There is nobody in literature who has stylistically so accurately transferred his understanding of boxing as he. That the world is unfair and that one may lose everything except one's self-respect and the dignity with which one learns to bear knockouts and injuries, Hemingway not only projected this world view onto bullfighting, soldiers at war and big game hunters but also put into the mouth of several boxers.*

Bertholt Brecht is definitely one of the great authors of the first half of the 20th Century. He wrote the memoirs of the sporting icon Samson Körner (from ship's boy to the amusement park boxer to German heavyweight champion), and was, in a manner of speaking, his biographer. The adventurous life story of a drifter who had emerged out of the twilight into the elite perfectly fitted the ideology of the time. In the same vein, Brecht's boxing novel *Das Renommee*, tells how a social outsider achieves fame thanks to his boxing skills – the novel with authentic scenes from the world championship title fight between Jack Dempsey and Georges Carpentier was never finished though. The successful novel *The Uppercut* instead tells the story of the downfall of a pro fighter. And also his *Plaque for 12 World Champions*, which chronicled the middleweight championship fight from 1891 to 1927, is a literary account of his own deeply held passion for boxing.

Although Brecht himself never set foot in the boxing ring, he remained an attentive observer; the world of boxing had a symbolic character for him. He portrayed society's class struggles as boxing duels.

In France, artists like Bracque, Matisse, Picasso or Rodin or Jean Cocteau barely missed a fight. And it is common knowledge that Jean-Paul Belmondo learned to box in the famous Avia Club in Issy les Moulineaux before acting meant that he no longer had time for it. Journalistic duty obliges us to also remember the film *Marcel and Edith* by the French director Claude Lelouch in which he describes the love affair between the boxer Marcel Cerdan and the world famous singer Edith Piaf.

21 Boxing
A sport for all

No matter what age, gender, background, education, income or social status you have, boxing in the form of boxercise or fitness boxing is a sport for you and a sport for all. There is a common perception that boxers must come from the slums of American suburbs, from the ghettos of African settlements, from Russian army barracks or from the high-rise apartment blocks of German cities. The idea of the sporting social climber who boxes his way out of poverty is very persistent. Stories of poor kids from the big city who have become multimillionaires due to their own hard work are too moving. This has actually been the case for a few famous boxers have, but team sport and track and field athletes have also had similar trajectories. It is the classic "rags to riches" story.

The idea that boxing is a good outlet for aggression, particularly for juvenile delinquents is equally persistent. It is true though that this sport demands exceptional discipline. Boxing is particularly valuable for young people, because by respecting their opponent he becomes a partner. It helps them to gain experience, character and maturity. Right from the first class, boxing therefore comprehensively offers just what is required, not only by those who are learning to deal with life, but by anyone who is looking for a healthy body and an enjoyable fitness experience.

More and more people are attending exercise classes and enjoying physical exertion. Boxing movements require great flexibility and mobility of the muscles and joints, making it an all-round fitness sport.

Because sports physicians and fitness trainers have long recognized this, fitness boxing classes are being offered more and more frequently in gyms, clubs and rehab centers. White Collar boxing, boxaerobics or move&box® classes are no longer the preserve of boxing clubs but punch bags can be found more and more often in gyms too. I have even seen them in the gyms of spas and in physical therapy centers.

Once the head area as a punching target is excluded from boxing training, which is the case as described in this book, the risk of injury is clearly reduced and almost eliminated. That is why the form of boxing training described here can also be recommended to those whose reactions are no longer as quick as they need to be in competitive boxing. Fitness boxing is even a great way of actually improving reaction speeds well into old age. Young and old can train together with no problem, and mixed classes are of course possible (as illustrated in this book) and make fitness fun.

Fitness boxing is also a form of exercise that should be included in the physical education program in schools as a matter of urgency. Boxing drills, punches, parries and their coordination with footwork are types of movement that school children lack in everyday life. The sport is also fun, boosts self-confidence, reduces aggression and improves limited motor skills.

Once you have developed an enjoyment of fitness boxing, you may want to keep it up wherever you are. That is why I always take two pairs of boxing mitts (boxing gloves with a stitched point on the palms) on vacation with me. With my wife, children and very often complete strangers who are interested in sports who happen to see me working out, I have experienced some wonderful training situations on vacation on the beach, in the hotel gym, on spontaneous visits to new gyms, sometimes even in the garden of guest houses, in the apartment lounge or wherever. I always bring my jump rope too, so that I am able to perform a complete workout comprising jumping rope, shadowboxing and partner boxing.

Boxing keeps you fit, boxing is a great fitness sport and is a real sport for all.

Young and old can participate together in an active and dynamic workout.

Index

Authors' Profiles

Andreas Riem

Sport is not just a part of his life; it IS his life. For many years he was active in combat sports, but these days he is more interested in fitness and exercise as a way of combining performance with physical well-being.

As a training consultant for a German Kickboxing Federation, of which he is also director, he uses his flair for sporting ideas to advise many gyms. This is also how his vision of a healthy recreational sport based on the elements of combat sports developed into the concept of move&box®. He has also drawn on the experience of running his own two gym.

He is multiple German champion of WAKO in kickboxing, took third place in the European Aerokickboxing championships and is a successful trainer of elite, recreational and fitness athletes.

Michael Kleymann

Michael Kleymann has been a sports journalist for over 30 years, he has been an editor, assistant and chief editor for various publishing houses and newspapers. He has also written several books, including some on kickboxing and boxing.

The author has always been passionate about practicing sports, particularly boxing, and he is a trainer of elite level youth boxers in his club and also trains kick boxers (he is WAKO licensed) and has established boxing as a recreational sport as a move&box® trainer in native town.

Move&box®

Concept:	Andreas Riem
Text:	Michael Kleymann
Photos:	Alexander Wittke, Michael Becker, Michael Kleymann (Chapter 5 and 16) gettyimages page 76
Contributors:	Bettina Krieger, Kim Sobkowiak, Dirk and Sandra Menzel, Sabine Seifert, Peter Trautwein
Equipment:	Paffen Sport
Cover Design:	Jens Vogelsang, Aachen

The Body Coach

Paul Collins
Power Training

For many years, coaches and athletes have sought to improve power, a combination of speed and strength, in order to enhance performance. Power Training is designed as an educational tool to assist in the development of training programs that aim to keep athletes fit, strong and powerful all year round.

136 pages, full-color print
247 photos
Paperback, $6^1/2$" x $9^1/4$"
ISBN: 978-1-84126-233-8
$ 14.95 US
£ 9.95 UK / € 14.95

Paul Collins
Core Strength

Core Strength features practical, easy-to-follow exercises to help you build your strongest body ever using your own body weight. The Body Coach, Paul Collins, provides step-by-step coaching with detailed descriptions of over 100 exercises.

About 144 pages, full-color print, 200 color photos
Paperback, $6^1/2$" x $9^1/4$"
ISBN: 978-1-84126-249-9
$ 14.95 US
£ 9.95 UK / € 14.95

Paul Collins
Awesome Abs

The abdominal muscles serve a critical function in daily movement, sport and physical activity. A strong midsection helps support and protect your lower back region from injury. Better Abs for All is packed with over 70 easy-to-follow exercises and tests aimed at achieving a leaner abdomen, a stronger lower back, better posture and a trimmer waistline.

136 pages, full-color print
229 photos &
4 illustrations
Paperback, $6^1/2$" x $9^1/4$"
ISBN: 978-1-84126-232-1
$ 14.95 US
£ 9.95 UK / € 14.95

Self-Defense

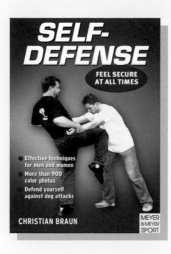

Christian Braun
Self-Defense

This self-help book is suitable for men and women of any age. Learn how to defend yourself against different types of attacks, from close combat attacks, fist fights, armed attacks or even dog attacks.
An experienced expert in self-defense and the martial arts leads you along a realistic route, showing how you can defend yourself at any time.

About 256 pages, full color print
935 color photos and illustrations
Paperback, 6^1/2" x 9^1/4"
ISBN: 978-1-84126-246-8
$ 19.95 US
£ 14.95 UK / € 19.95

Christian Braun
Self-Defense against Knife Attacks

Techniques for the defense against knife attacks are not only of interest for martial artists of various disciplines. Everyone who is looking for effective ways to defend himself against these attacks in all kinds of situations will find detailed instructions in this book.

288 pages, full-color print
1700 photos and illustrations
Paperback, 6^1/2" x 9^1/4"
ISBN: 978-1-84126-198-0
$ 19.95 US
£ 14.95 UK / € 18.95

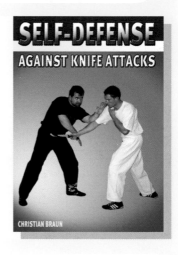

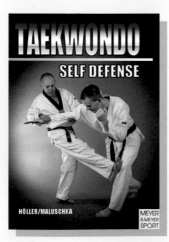

Höller/Maluschka
Taekwondo – Self-Defense

This book presents the best Taekwondo techniques and train-ing forms in order to effectively learn self-defense. This allows not only for a successful promotion test in the domain of self-defense but also for a greate chance of successfully responding to dangerous situations in everyday life.

224 pages, full-color print
217 photos and 8 illustrations
Paperback, 5^3/4" x 8^1/4"
ISBN: 978-1-84126-134-8
$ 17.95 US
£ 12.95 UK / € 18.90

www.m-m-sports.com

MEYER & MEYER SPORT